Sport
Faith
Life

CALVIN SHORTS

Sport
Faith
Life

by Brian R. Bolt

CALVIN COLLEGE • PRESS

Grand Rapids, MI • calvin.edu/press

Published 2018 by the Calvin College Press
3201 Burton St. SE
Grand Rapids, MI 49546

Scripture quotations are from the Holy Bible, New International Version®. NIV®. Copyright © 1973, 1978, 1984, 2011 by Biblica, Inc.™ Used by permission of Zondervan. All rights reserved worldwide. www.zondervan.com. The "NIV" and "New International Version" are trademarks registered in the United States Patent and Trademark Office by Biblica, Inc.™

Publisher's Cataloging-in-Publication Data

Names: Bolt, Brian R., author.
Title: Sport. faith. life. / Brian R. Bolt.
Series: Calvin Shorts.
Description: Includes bibliographical references. | Grand Rapids, MI: Calvin College Press, 2018.
Identifiers: ISBN 978-1-937555-30-6 (pbk.) | 978-1-937555-31-3 (ebook)
LCCN 2018943502
Subjects: LCSH Sports--Religious aspects--Christianity. | Christian life. | BISAC RELIGION / Christian Life / General | SPORTS & RECREATION / General
Classification: LCC GV706.42 .B65 2018| DDC 796.01--dc23

Cover design: Robert Alderink
Interior design and typeset: Katherine Lloyd, The DESK

The Calvin College Press has no responsibility for the persistence or accuracy of URLs for external or third-party internet websites referred to in this publication and does not guarantee that any content on such websites is, or will remain, accurate or appropriate.

Contents

Series Editor's Foreword

Midway along the journey of our life
I woke to find myself in some dark woods,
For I had wandered off from the straight path.

So begins *The Divine Comedy*, a classic meditation on the Christian life, written by Dante Alighieri in the fourteenth century.

Dante's three images—a journey, a dark forest, and a perplexed pilgrim—still feel familiar today, don't they?

We can readily imagine our own lives as a series of journeys: not just the big journey from birth to death, but also all the little trips from home to school, from school to job, from place to place, from old friends to new. In fact, we often feel we are simultaneously on multiple journeys that tug us in diverse and sometimes opposing directions. We recognize those dark woods from fairy tales and nightmares and the all-too-real conundrums that crowd our everyday lives. No wonder we frequently feel perplexed. We wake up shaking our heads, unsure if we know how to live wisely today or tomorrow or next week.

This series has in mind just such perplexed pilgrims. Each book invites you, the reader, to walk alongside experienced guides who will help you understand the contours of the road as well as the surrounding landscape. They will cut back the underbrush, untangle myths and misconceptions, and suggest ways to move forward.

And they will do it in books intended to be read in an evening or during a flight. Calvin Shorts are designed not just for perplexed pilgrims but also for busy ones. We live in a complex and changing world. We need nimble ways to acquire knowledge, skills, and wisdom. These books are one way to meet those needs.

John Calvin, after whom this series is named, recognized our pilgrim condition. "We are always on the road," he said, and although this road, this life, is full of perplexities, it is also "a gift of divine kindness which is not to be refused." Calvin Shorts takes as its starting point this claim that we are called to live well in a world that is both gift and challenge.

In *The Divine Comedy*, Dante's guide is Virgil, a wise but not omniscient mentor. So, too, the authors in the Calvin Shorts series don't pretend to know it all. They, like you and me, are pilgrims. And they invite us to walk with them as together we seek to live more faithfully in this world that belongs to God.

Susan M. Felch
Executive Editor
The Calvin College Press

Additional Resources

Additional online resources for *Sport. Faith. Life.* may be available at www.calvin.edu/press.

Additional information, references, and citations are included in the notes at the end of this book. Rather than using footnote numbers, the comments are keyed to phrases and page numbers.

Acknowledgments

My love of sport always seemed built in, and my mom and dad were keen enough to recognize it early. They nurtured it with rides to ball games, needed equipment, and being sure not to miss the sign-up dates for sport seasons. I am grateful for this, but more so for the way they framed sport within a Christian home. They followed, supported, and encouraged while never making too much or too little of my sport interests, achievements, or failures. With no formal expertise, they seemed to have an easy sense of how sport can either enhance or consume life. And because of their grounding in an authentic Christian faith, they navigated my sport experiences like seasoned veterans. I still go to them often for advice about sport, faith, and life.

There are many additional resources available that provide a more thorough analysis of sport. Some of these are listed at the end of this book. I am very grateful to these authors who have helped me think better about sport. I am also thankful for those who prayed with and for me through this process, and for those who encouraged me to continue writing, especially when I questioned whether I actually had anything of value to say. Val Gin of Gordon College helped me form the concept and overall scope of this book. Expert suggestions came from my longtime friend, former sport teammate, and now athletic director Jim Timmer, Jr., my theologian colleague Matt Lundberg, and the book's sharp-thinking editor, Susan Felch. Chad Carlson, a sport philosopher and surprisingly trusted colleague from a rival institution, chipped in with equal parts scholarly advice and practical encouragement. Dale Williams patiently helped me sort through needed publishing and design details. And I could not have written this book without Natalie Hubers, who works in my office. Natalie reads everything I write with a keen eye, but more importantly, with a willing and perceptive heart. She has invested in my work much more than I deserve, and for that, I am very grateful.

Finally, my beloved wife, Joni, and children, Grace, Maria, and George, have humored my interests and were unknowing subjects in the laboratory where this book was born. Sport is a part of our Christian home, more or less with each passing year. My joy in sport—playing and watching—is most often with them. To all, thanks for playing.

What
Is Sport?

1

I would rather play or watch sports than write about them. Although you have opened this book, I suspect you would say the same about reading it. Sport isn't just something we read about. It is something we do.

Sport attracts both young and old from all around the world. Recently, I was in Malawi, Africa, with a group of college students. We visited several villages in the Great Rift Valley. None of us spoke Chichewa. None of the villagers felt comfortable speaking English. So each time we arrived in a village, we simply kicked a soccer ball around in an open space. One, two, or three at a time, boys and girls gathered until there were dozens of village kids around us. The adults followed. A kick toward our onlookers brought beaming smiles—and a return pass. Without prompting, the young Malawians started to make more sophisticated moves with the ball, using different parts of their feet and legs to trap, juggle, and pass. Instinctively, we all moved closer together. We started contesting passes, and we positioned our bodies to keep the ball protected from those who might take it. Alliances, loose boundaries, and rules about contact and space formed organically. The beaming smiles became clenched faces that expressed determination, exasperation, and self-satisfaction. Sport was bubbling up from the earth. We were all caught in its current.

Our experience in Malawi was not unique. Most people interact with sport in some capacity, and most do so directly. From toddlers to seniors, people play sports in backyards, vacant lots, or structured environments such as schools, YMCAs, private clubs, churches, nonprofit centers, or municipal parks. Fans watch games on television and devices, in massive stadiums, or from bleachers and folding chairs.

Sport absorbs our families, media and social media, careers, schools, and sometimes even our worship spaces. If we don't love sport, we can try to tolerate, hate, or ignore it, but we cannot eliminate it. Sport has staying power. Through war and peace, poverty and prosperity, sport indiscriminately captures our hearts. It draws new and unsuspecting converts daily.

The word *sport* is used as a root for nouns, adjectives, and verbs and can refer to various types of activities. But this book addresses what most of us think of first: a contest or set of contests between teams or individuals involving some type of physical skill and exertion. For instance, in this book, bass fishing is not considered a sport, but a bass fishing tournament in which teams compete to catch the most and biggest fish in a period of time is. The contest itself also needs to have some semblance of equality and purpose. A game between two competing high school varsity teams may end with a lopsided score, but at least the teams were both trying to win. Conversely, when my extended family clears a patch of ice on a lake to play broomball, the game has elements of sport, but since the ages on the ice range from six to sixty, the game is more recreational than pure sport.

Since many of us experience sport in one way or another, we may think about it as either positive or negative. As is often the case, it is not that simple. In fact, thinking about sport as simply good or bad may be misleading.

Consider two retired, very successful, high-profile athletes who are almost the same age: Mariano Rivera and Lance Armstrong. Both athletes set records and distinguished themselves as the best in the world at their sports. Rivera was the closer for the New York Yankees for seventeen years and holds the record for the most career saves in Major League Baseball history (652). Lance Armstrong won the prestigious Tour de France bicycle race a record seven times. But all seven wins were voided due to his use of illegal performance enhancing drugs and blood doping techniques. Both Rivera and Armstrong spent years honing their crafts, interacting with teammates, experiencing success and failure, learning and training with the best coaches, and pushing themselves to perform at their best in high-pressure situations. Yet Rivera is known for his accomplishments, humility, and integrity. Armstrong is known for cheating and lying. With such opposite reputations for such similar men, what are we to make of sport?

We don't need extreme examples such as Rivera and Armstrong to recognize the double-edged sword of sport.

We know that sport comes with both merits and snares. It offers the opportunity to develop talent and skills. It also tempts us to make wrong choices. The point is not to label Rivera a saint and Armstrong a sinner. Instead, it is to admit out loud what we know in our minds, our hands, and our hearts. The experience of sport is complex, and whether sport is played on the public stage or in a vacant field, it has great potential for both good and evil—in society at large and for individuals.

Among the many sport participants and spectators are confessing Christians, people who view life as a gift of God's grace and earnestly desire to follow Jesus Christ in their day-to-day activities. Many Christians have grown to understand sport and Christianity to be as compatible as peanut butter and jelly. How could they not work together? But the unquestioned compatibility is actually a recent phenomenon. The Christian church has a well-documented history of suspicion toward sport and has often wondered whether Christians should be involved in sport at all, a question still worth considering.

Yet today's Christians are less likely to ban sport or withdraw from it. Most participate willingly and focus on the positive aspects of sport, but with underlying anxieties stemming from their day-to-day decisions. Are sports too dangerous? Is there such a thing as being too competitive? Does winning really matter? What is the point of sports? Should I force my child to play organized sports? Is my daughter getting a fair chance to play? Should I approach the high school coach with my concerns or stay quiet? Should I play in my championship soccer game or go to church? Why do I hate losing so much? Is travel baseball a poor use of resources? Was that a "dirty" play?

As Christians, we may also move beyond these immediate concerns to wonder about the habits, affections, and passions that sport cultivates in individuals and in society. We wrestle with our own hearts, gripped by the joys and obsessions of competition, and we wonder why it is that sport can seem both underutilized and overdone at the same time. With sport scandals in every news report, we worry about the physical and emotional safety of sporting environments. Perhaps we recognize the unequal opportunities in sport based on zip codes and family income, and we see rampant corruption seemingly built into some sport systems and cultures. We lament over poor players who are pushed aside and excellent performers who are pushed ahead, all seemingly serving the self-interest of those in positions of power.

The goal for this short book is not to answer all these questions but rather to look carefully at them and provide an understanding of sport that helps all of us make wise decisions. Of course, my own views are shaped by my background. I am a Protestant Christian white male living in the United States who just turned fifty and who both loves and makes his living in the world of sport. Although my scope is limited, I hope you, the reader, will find commonalities with your own experiences, whatever they may be. What we share is the desire to understand and play sports within the context of a full and rich Christian life. We want to be disciples of Jesus Christ in our sport as well as in every other area of our lives.

Ahead, Chapter 2 gets to the heart of sport, identifying it as an experience similar to other activities but unique in its own way. Chapter 3 takes a step back to look at how the Christian church has interacted with sport in history and outlines how to make sense of sport through the Bible and Christian wisdom. Competition is central to sport, with all its possibilities and pitfalls, so Chapter 4 explains competition and explores how Christians may need to look at it from a fresh perspective. Finally, Chapters 5 and 6 take a look at how an authentic understanding of sport can help Christians discern wisdom from foolishness, helping all of us experience sport as a part of this good, fallen, and redeemed world.

The Experience
of Sport

2

YOU HAD TO BE THERE

A story is told about the famous composer Ludwig von Beethoven, who at a dinner party was asked by the host to play something. He agreed, sat down at the piano, and played a beautiful piece from beginning to end. The guests were in awe. One woman spoke up, asking, "Sir, that was the most beautiful thing I've ever heard. Can you tell me what it means?" The composer said nothing. He simply sat down at the piano and played the entire piece over again, then left in silence.

Experiences such as listening to a beautiful piece of music are understandably hard to explain, and some wonder why we even try, because the meaning *is* the experience. The *experience* is why people listen to music. It is also why people read stories, watch movies, visit art museums, and travel to exotic places. And the *experience* is why people play sports. For all these activities, there are other motives and other goods to be gained, but it is the experience itself that beckons us. We may attempt to think about our experiences, or to explain them, but for some reason, when we try to fully reproduce the moment, our words fall short—and maybe that is how it was meant to be. When we recount sport stories to each other, whether about our own or others' fantastic performances or failures, we finally get frustrated and exclaim, "I guess you just had to be there!" *There* is where sport happens, and the true value of *there* is in the experience itself.

The sport experience is one of wonder and strain, imagination and ingenuity, hope and despair. The pull of sport can be a single moment or a near lifetime of focused effort. Sport is often compared with music, art, theater, and even religious practice. Sport, like these experiences, can be all-encompassing. But sport is not a song, a painting, or a literary work, and though the sport culture is full of ritual and ceremony, sport is not a religion. Part of understanding sport and finding a place for it in a Christian life requires understanding what it is and what it isn't. Finding this place does not mean sport is void of significance or is strictly secular. Like all human experiences, sport provides an opportunity for celebrating the prospects and the limits of humans created in God's image.

IT JUST DOESN'T MATTER

For a long time, scholars did not bother to explore or study sport at all since it was generally considered frivolous, without meaning, and unworthy of serious attention. They were wrong, but they were also on to something. The sports we enjoy playing and watching aren't *actually* serious or meaningful in the same way that getting married, having children, finding a job, or being a disciple of Jesus Christ is serious and meaningful. The twist is this: the importance of sport is really its *unimportance*.

I am embarrassed to admit how much I like to follow some professional teams from Detroit, Michigan. I am a homegrown fan, indoctrinated by familiar play-by-play voices on the radio and the different shades of blue of the Tigers, Lions, and Pistons. For me, those three teams provide 365 days of tortured delight. When one season ends, another begins, with the rare overlap of pivotal games on the same day. The thought of a "big game tonight" buoys my workdays and elevates my spirit with irrational hope. Winning and championships are almost as elusive as a sighting of Bigfoot, yet I continue trudging through the woods with my eyes peeled. I have a permanent ticket on the proverbial bandwagon and appropriate disdain for those who jump on when it picks up speed. Time spent—time marvelously wasted. For me, sport is the most important of unimportant things.

The word *sport* itself comes from the medieval English word *desport*, meaning "a diversion or escape from serious matters." At its best, sport does carry us away into another world. In that way, it is like music, and theater, and storytelling. All these activities are in one sense "unimportant." They are not necessary to feed, clothe, and house us. But they are a natural part of a full human life if we are to develop our imaginative, physical, and creative potential. Sport, for instance, allows us to enter a mythical world, complete with flashy costumes, task-specific weapons of combat, fantastic venues, obscure rules, and compelling narratives. To participate in sport, whether as spectator or player, is like walking through the wardrobe with Peter, Susan, Edmund, and Lucy into the land of Narnia that C. S. Lewis created. The mythical rules and boundaries of sport cast us, just like the Pevensie children, on an alternative stage, and we are the actors playing ourselves. Our names don't change, but the focus of our interest does. We rightly become absorbed in the game, discovering and creating as needed in an ever-changing environment. In one sense, this playacting is unimportant. In another sense, it is part of what makes us human beings.

NOTHING ELSE MATTERS

Although we might agree that sport is a diversion, that "it just doesn't matter," we also recognize how powerful play-acting can be. The unimportance of sport is intimately linked to the fact that it simultaneously demands serious attention, allegiance, and a desire to be better.

We can give much or little of ourselves to the make-be-lieve world of sport, but the more engaged we become, the better the experience. Part of sport's allure is that it makes a sharp detour from amusing recreation and boldly requires a sincere encounter. When a group of friends are shooting hoops at a park and a decision is made to start a game, something changes. If just one of those friends doesn't want to play, decides not to try very hard to guard his opponent, or just acts goofy, he is labeled a spoilsport. The player's nonseriousness has actually spoiled the experience.

Serious attention in sport forms temporary connections among teammates. And affiliating with a team, as a player or a fan, can create some pretty tenacious bonds. I recently traveled to a friend's wedding in Tuscaloosa, Alabama, the home of his soon-to-be bride. In planning the wedding, the couple considered two possible weekends. One weekend meant the groom's sister would not be able to attend due to another wedding commitment for her college roommate. The other weekend the bride's family would have to miss a University of Alabama football game. The result was predictable: the groom's sister watched the wedding from a distance on her phone. Sport provides many of us with a sense of belonging. This belonging or connection can be very strong when it comes to forming identity and making day-to-day decisions, for better or for worse (wedding pun intended). *Roll Tide.*

Sport not only grabs our serious attention and allegiance but also demands a desire for excellence, a desire to be better. To be clear, a person does not need to be excellent to play sports. For most, excellence cannot be objectively quantified; sport excellence is actually quite relative. A great sprinter from a small-town high school track team may not even be able to beat the slowest runner on a team at a larger school in the city. At home, she is excellent; down the road, she is ordinary. Excellence is always measured by comparison, and the target is elusive. Of course, most of us never reach excellence by any standard in sport, but that is not the point. The point is we must try.

I coach an intercollegiate golf team. I am constantly coaching my players to do something they have never done, to perform better than they have in the past. As college athletes, they are already elite performers, but they are also perpetually unsatisfied with their ability and performance—and I need them to be unsatisfied. They know that shooting a 69 or hitting a 50-foot putt for eagle does not happen very often, yet they try every time out. On the field or off, sport can bring us satisfaction, but we are never truly satisfied.

Competitors strive for something better because it is part of the craft of sport. Craft is not only about the movements of hands and feet. Craft also involves studied strategy, discerning vision, and a knack to be in the right place when it matters most. For athletes, there is a point in sport when the game slows down, when movements become intuitive. Decisions are made as if there is foreknowledge of what an opponent will do. Unlike theater, sport has no script, so improvisation and the ability to produce an already learned skill at the moment of greatest pressure is often the difference between acclaim and anguish. Craft can also apply to nonplayers. An educated spectator sees what others do not. He or she understands how just a small tilt of the head at the right time can change the outcome of a contest. Everyone can cheer when the thrills are obvious, but an expert sees smaller moments of artistry shared by only a few.

Attention, allegiance, and a desire to be better make sport an unimportant but utterly serious human endeavor.

So do personal feelings of pleasure and accomplishment. Sport takes us where we are, with our own unique interests and personalities. For some, an occasional game of tennis with a friend fills the need, while others spend hours staring at a black line on the bottom of a pool, laboring to take just one-hundredth of a second off a record freestyle time. One player loves the feeling of a perfect touch against a soccer ball—when the instep meets the air-pressured sphere so precisely that she doesn't need to see it fly. She knows its path will be spot-on. Another person loves the "thwop" sound of the badminton birdie on a smash, and still another finds pleasure in the full-body strain of pushing the pile on the rugby pitch. For me as a baseball player, I would add perfectly shucking a sunflower seed with just my mouth and wearing my hat just a little off-center.

There is just something right about those good feelings in sport. And we will look at them more carefully in Chapter 3, when we consider the nature of "play." But the experience of sport also raises some serious challenges.

SHOW ME THE MONEY

In the movie *Jerry Maguire*, the title character plays a sport agent frustrated with his football-star client Rod Tidwell. Maguire says to Tidwell, "Right now, you are a paycheck player. You play with your head, not your heart." People often lament the role of money in sport. They get angry over greedy professional team owners, obscene player salaries, and expensive ticket prices. Somehow, the money seems like a violation, an affront to what sport is supposed to be. Intuitively, we know that sport is about the experience, so it seems stained and made less pure by the introduction of money. Most of us go to work every day, and we probably would live very different lives if we didn't need the paycheck that goes with it. But sport doesn't need money. Sport has its own prize called victory, which we will address more in Chapter 4.

The truth, however, is that money has always been a part of sport. For example, most people know that winning athletes in ancient Greece earned a laurel wreath crown, but they might not know that athletes also received huge monetary prizes. The games and ceremonies lasted for weeks, and since many people came, the games were big moneymakers for local merchants. Today, fans of sport pay hundreds of dollars for good seats at marquee events, and as a parent, I pay five dollars each time to watch my kids play high school sports. Families will often pay for prestigious travel teams, and, though the names will change, interested teens will pay for Lebron James shoes. Money means sport opportunity for those who have it and exclusion for those who don't. But through foundations, donations, grants, and government resources, money also funds civic and nonprofit organizations around the world that provide sport experiences to those in need. When it comes to sport for self and others, people are often willing to reach for their wallets.

Money is not evil, but the love of it is. Many will argue that money ruins sport, but it is more accurate to say that money changes sport. A friend of mine has a daughter who was advancing quickly by age ten in the sport of power tumbling and gymnastics. At a very young age, she was a graceful and powerful athlete, doing what she loved, pushing herself to perform new and better acrobatic stunts. What she could do with her body in the air would make most of us cringe with fear and gasp with astonishment. She enjoyed competing, affiliating with her gym, and traveling to new places. Her talent led to opportunity: phone calls came in from coaches with promises of scholarships or access to elite training programs and the prospect of endorsements. But in her case, things didn't go too well from there. Her performance suffered, and her injuries mounted. Eventually, it was clear she was not going to be the elite performer that some thought she would be. The pressure to earn money increased, and the desire to achieve became the need to perform. For her, sport was becoming a job.

When sport is played mostly for prestige, or a university scholarship, or even as a professional means of income, it requires the athlete to do some mental and emotional gymnastics. People in professional sport media complain that players don't seem to give them honest responses to questions. They want raw quotes about winning and losing and earning big contracts, but players and coaches often respond with clichés such as "We're just trying to get better every day" or "We just take one day at a time." These players are not lying or avoiding the media—or, at least, that is not all they are doing. Instead, they have learned to hold the external benefits of sport at bay by focusing on the fun and the processes of the game as they did when they first started playing. They intuitively know that a preoccupied focus on external rewards is actually detrimental to sport success. Most of us don't have jobs that originated in our childhood play, but professional athletes do, and the essence of sport requires them to play seriously, as if sport doesn't matter at all.

THE BEAST OF BURDEN

Besides money, other goods and causes are often draped over sport like that ill-fitting sweater Grandma gave you for Christmas. My wife and I once purchased a weekend trip to an exotic resort for a cheap price. The only requirement for getting such a good deal was that we had to attend a ninety-minute seminar about purchasing vacation property on the resort. We were there for a vacation, not to buy property, but the seminar was part of the deal. Many of you will recognize this as the standard "time-share tactic," a method of sales that uses the attraction of a sandy beach and luxurious accommodations to lure people in to hear a forced, often high-pressured sales pitch. Sport is very popular, and it is no wonder that much like the time-share tactic, people will use the popularity of sport to coerce other actions out of people or to advertise messages that are not at all connected to the sport experience.

In 2016, NFL quarterback Colin Kaepernick started a movement by kneeling during the playing of the USA national anthem prior to a football game, not unlike Tommie Smith and John Carlos at the 1968 Olympics years before. My point here is not to join the conversation about the merits of Kaepernick's action but to illustrate how sport became tangled up in the debate. Kaepernick's kneeling was a form of protest, but not toward the game of football. Kaepernick was using a time-share tactic. He knew that he could get his message out to the greatest number of people by using the attraction of the country's most popular sport. Ironically, he was protesting during the national anthem, which in some ways is a time-share tactic of its own. Playing the national anthem prior to athletic competition became a regular practice during World War II, when officials considered it a good way to foster patriotism. In neither case was the cause about sport. Instead, people used the allure of sport to gain attention for a particular message. Regardless of your view of Kaepernick's protest or the playing of the national anthem, in both cases the practice brought substantive real-life issues into the world of sport. If sport is at its heart its own experience, a diversion from the weighty matters of life—if it is a form of make-believe in which we can truly invest ourselves but without real-life consequences—we can understand the frustration with either forced patriotism or opportunistic protest.

The most attractive and popular sports will always carry a burden beyond themselves. Many of those causes will be good, which is why sport is so often connected to education, including Christian education through schools and churches. Innumerable books, blogs, and personal testimonies tell of the powerful and positive impact of sport on human lives. One of my boyhood heroes, Kirk Gibson, who played college football and baseball and went on to legendary status in Major League Baseball, now has Parkinson's disease. Gibby says he is attacking it as an athlete. He is battling hard against the disease, competing against it, as he learned on the field. These stories uplift and inspire us. Yet it is important to remember that opposite stories also exist. Some athletes don't attack disease; they attack other people, including their wives and children.

There is actually little evidence that sport by itself builds character or fosters Christian faith. In fact, sport may have the opposite effect. This doesn't make Gibby's story less true, nor does it mean that other stories of recovery, liberation, or learning through sport are unhelpful. But it reminds us that there are always parts to the story that we don't know. We should not attribute too much credit or blame to sport. As is the case with most things, the devil (and God) is in the details.

The news headlines of the day constantly remind us of sin and its by-products. People lie, cheat, steal, kill, and commit sexual sins. Not surprisingly, sport headlines are often similar, because sports are played, managed, and marketed by people, all of whom are as susceptible to wrongdoing as everyone else. At the highest levels, temptation for cutting corners, cheating, exploitation, and cover-up often reaches a fever pitch. Winning often requires money, and money is often the result of winning, so the two feed each other, sometimes in corrupt ways. The goodness of sport, as part of the world that God has created, does not mean it has a layer of protection from the corruptive and corrosive power of sin.

We love sport and are attracted to it in ways we often cannot explain, but because of its allure, there is a great temptation to harness sport, requiring it to pull a load it often cannot bear. When sport is played primarily for something other than the experience itself, be it external rewards such as money or fame, or formative attributes such as character or Christian faith, sport becomes a knock-off version of its true essence.

WHOLE AND BROKEN

Sport grips our whole selves. Schools have a subject called physical education, but sport is hardly just physical. Sport penetrates our being. In the times we are engaged, it feasts on our mental and emotional energy, getting more from us than we imagine possible. But because it is also physical, sport involves something that other experiences do not, namely the body. The discipline of the athlete was something that caught the apostle Paul's attention. He could see the tenacity and dedication in sport and how athletes were sold out toward their prize, in their heads, feet, and hearts. Paul was not necessarily endorsing sport as an activity, but he was recognizing its uniqueness in engaging the whole person.

At age forty-eight, I took up the sport of pickleball. If you are unfamiliar with it, it is like tennis only played on a smaller court with a paddle and a plastic ball. The game can be played indoors or outdoors, mostly in doubles format, and it is becoming very popular all over the world. After playing with some friends, learning some skills, and getting a beginning understanding of the strategy, a friend and I decided to enter a tournament. We didn't really know what to expect, and we soon found ourselves in the losers' bracket and forced to play several games in a row without rest. In all, my partner and I played about five straight hours, getting to the championship game. It was brilliant, and I allowed myself to get caught up in the drama. About halfway through the final game, I felt a sharp twinge in my left knee. With only a few points between us and the championship, I pressed on, and we won!

A few days later, I was recovering from knee surgery. I had torn the meniscus on both sides of my knee. Now my MRI picture hangs in my office next to the small gold medal we won at the pickleball tournament, which probably cost about three dollars. I hobbled around for about three months after surgery, and it seems as if another medical bill comes in the mail every day. The objective observer rightly concludes that playing that long, and playing to the finish, was unwise. I don't disagree. But oddly, I must admit, I would probably do it again.

In Chapter 6, we will talk further about wisdom and foolishness in sport. But here I simply want to acknowledge how important our bodies are to God as part of his creation. Scripture takes great pains to describe human bodies: Sampson was strong, Eli was fat, Saul was tall, Zacchaeus was short, Ehud was left-handed, and Job's daughters and Rachel were beautiful. We are all on a continuum of ability and disability, physically, mentally, emotionally, spiritually. Jesus addressed all aspects of the human condition. He healed lepers, gave working legs to the lame, and stopped continuous bleeding. He also exorcised the mad, educated the confused, and calmed the anxious. At the same time, Jesus's friends did not live perfect lives. Peter continued to struggle with his temper, Martha kept on worrying, and Paul endured his thorn. Our bodies are both whole, because God created them good, and broken, because of our own continuing sin.

God works his plan of redemption through the ups and downs of our ordinary lives as we learn to trust God, obey his Word, and discern between wisdom and foolishness. The whole experience of sport—its unimportance and significance; its calls for attention, allegiance, and excellence; its temptations to abuse money and prestige; its pain and injury—sets the stage on which we see God keeping his promise to redeem us as we respond to his grace and gentle correction. In the playacting that is sport, we have an opportunity to practice "being Christian," not simply doing Christian things. And being Christian is both much harder and more rewarding than doing Christian things, as we shall see in the following chapters.

Sport and
the Church

3

SAME AS IT EVER WAS

Sport has a universal appeal, and it always has. Every culture in human history has included play in some form or another, and many times that form could be labeled sport. The ancient Mayans played a game with a ball and a horizontal hoop, while swordplay and a game similar to soccer were popular in China. The Olympic Games of Greece began in 776 BC and continued for more than one thousand years, even after Rome conquered its territory. Medieval knights honed their skills in jousting tournaments. In the thirteenth century, the Dutch fixed metal blades to their shoes for skating matches on the frozen canals. Most of the sports we recognize today were organized and given common rules in the eighteenth and nineteenth centuries, and their popularity continues to grow.

In modern society, one way to track interest in sport is by following the money. The current estimated global market for the sport industry is 1.3 trillion American dollars, mostly connected to the 4 billion people who participate in and follow soccer. In North America, the sport market in 2014 was $60.5 billion, and it is expected to eclipse $73 billion by 2019. This money is not all reserved for big-time corporate sport and player salaries. The youth market in the United States alone, which includes things such as merchandising, equipment, private coaching, travel, and tournament organization, was a $15.3 billion market in 2017, a 55 percent increase from 2010.

With all its dollars and attention, it is no wonder that sport has drawn the eye of the Christian church. Since ancient times, the church has kept watch on sport, often not knowing exactly what to make of it. Sport and the sacred were often corkscrewed within each other. That ball game in Central America was actually a religious ritual that honored the gods of the underworld. It is possible that after the game some participants were sacrificed and their severed skulls were used to make the ball. The crown games of Greece were pagan festivals that lasted weeks at a time, each celebrating a different god. Zeus earned the honors in Olympia and Nemea, while Apollo and Poseidon were honored in Delphi and Corinth. The Greek goddess of victory, Nike, lives on today through the sport equipment company that bears her name.

It is no wonder that the early church set out to untangle sport from matters of faith. Church leaders sometimes agreed that sport had a place in society, possibly for good health or safe recreation. There was also the occasional sermon illustration, thanks to Paul and his regular use of sport analogies. But the Greek games had morphed into fantastic public spectacles in Rome, complete with chariot races and bloody gladiator contests. The church's interest in sport quickly changed to suspicion. There were concerns about the idolatrous culture, youth formation, and Sabbath keeping. Prohibitions and bans were issued. For instance, in AD 314, at the first Council of Arles, church members were forbidden, upon threat of excommunication, from fraternizing with gladiators and charioteers. When Christianity became the official religion of the empire, the Olympic Games were officially ended by Theodosius I in AD 391 due to their pagan origins.

The warnings and prohibitions persisted well into the next several centuries. For instance, the sport of medieval Europe included jousting tournaments by knights in shining armor who would try to win the hands of fair maidens. As can be expected, these festivals had their own flavor of debauchery and distraction. They were scorned by Christian leaders for luring men away from church attendance and later from their duties in crusades. Yet not surprisingly, the power and popularity of sport won out. When people were faced with a choice between following the church's decrees or participating in sport, sport always proved too powerful, especially for men. Recognizing loss of attendance and allegiance, the church reluctantly switched course and reconsidered its position on the sport of the day. The church was recognizing that sport was a force to be reckoned with.

GIMME THAT SOBER MIRTH

In the sixteenth century, the Reformation altered the Christian landscape in Europe, forcing a separation among Christians and a radical change of religious practices among the new Protestants. Some English Christians with ties to Calvinism found their way to the Americas and established colonies that sought to give clear and simple guidelines for the Christian life. They held the Bible in high regard and strove to apply biblically based moral standards to all aspects of life, including amusements such as sport.

Much later, these Puritans were labeled the "fun police," a reputation they did not fully earn. While it is true that the Puritans promoted a disciplined life and valued work, they also recognized that totally removing recreation and sport from the lives of parishioners was unwise. Much of their criticism of sport was not about the amusements themselves but about abuses. They worried that the aristocratic class preferred play to work, that sport sometimes conflicted with Sabbath observance, and that certain sports promoted gambling. Puritans did not set out to remove sport. In some cases, however, they did develop a robust list of rules to determine whether an activity was appropriate. This somewhat legalistic and utilitarian tone is summed up in the Puritan concept of "sober mirth," which referred to a kind of restrained enjoyment. Sober mirth may sound dull to our modern ears, but we can thank the Puritans for caring enough about leisure activities such as sport to study and map out how and when sport may be an important part of a Christian community.

In the Puritan community, like many others before and after, the choice between godly living and lively sport was an easy one for those on the fence. The power of sport won again, so the church made accommodations. Church leaders did not want to defend limitations on fun in sport, yet they still believed that to give in purely to pleasure was a slippery slope. So the church began to leverage sport for its own purposes, opening the door for a movement called "Muscular Christianity." This movement began in England and America in the mid-nineteenth century. It coupled Christian discipleship with physical development, largely through sport. Appealing strongly to males, the theory was that the toughness, grit, and perseverance of sport trained the modern Christian to fight for Christ. The Young Men's Christian Association (YMCA), which once was opposed to sport, became a leader in developing the church's altered position. During this period, many sports developed consistent rules and regulations so that competition could spread from one population to another. The Muscular Christianity movement, in fact, fueled the rapid expansion of sport into the twentieth century.

This very brief and selective recounting of the church and sport paints a limited picture, but it does highlight the church's changing position on sport and reveals how the two have been in a battle for the hearts of Christians. Because the world had connected sport to pagan worship, and because sport was distracting attention from matters of faith, the church was right to be suspicious. Though the church's attempts to accommodate sport through the years have been more practical than theological, the church was working to make sense of sport in each new environment. Recent biblical study and a developing theology of sport provide a more nuanced view and help us find a secure place for sport in the Christian life.

Though the language has changed, the modern church has not radically shifted its perspective since the era of Muscular Christianity. No longer is sport the enemy lurking around the corner. Muscular Christianity made it okay, or even necessary, for Christians to participate in the sport culture. Over the past half century, large-scale Christian sport organizations have emerged, such as Athletes in Action, Fellowship of Christian Athletes, and the now vast network of sport chaplaincy organizations around the world. Dozens of smaller Christian sport organizations have also sprung up throughout the world. These organizations focus on evangelism, discipleship, or pastoral care in and through sport. Sport has also drawn the attention of the Catholic Church. Pope Francis has called sport "a human activity of great value, able to enrich people's lives." In response, the Vatican launched "Sport in the Service of Humanity," a large-scale effort to explore the potential of sport for the common good. All suspicion is not gone, but while some Christians continue to debate the ethics of sport and the moral implications of its importance in culture, most clergy from all Christian faith traditions focus on meeting people where they are and highlighting the positive aspects of sport.

PARADISE LOST AND FOUND

Organized sport existed in both Old and New Testament times, but if the Bible were a newspaper, you would notice there isn't a sports section. As with many other things not specifically addressed in Scripture, we are left to explore larger themes in an effort to determine God's will for our approach to sport. To do so, let's begin with an old problem, the separation of human persons into two parts, mind and body. The church has grappled many times with the difficulties this dualism raises.

Though most Christians expect to be temporarily separated from their bodies at death, Scripture clearly affirms the value of the body. God himself lovingly made our bodies from the dust of the earth. The Holy Spirit claims our bodies now as his temple. God promises that we will one day live as resurrected bodies, not as disembodied immortal souls.

Spiritual and physical redemption are linked in the incarnation of Jesus Christ. The flesh Jesus took on was well worn by the time he left the earth. His body was starved in the desert and torn to shreds on the cross, but along the way, he had dinner with friends, made wine, consoled the brokenhearted, and walked on water. We have no evidence that Jesus played sports, but we also don't know if he played an instrument, painted pictures, or balanced a checkbook. We do know that he reappeared to the disciples in bodily form and ascended the same way. And we know that he will come again to finish his work in us, transforming us into glorious heavenly bodies the grandeur of which we can only imagine. The wholeness of humans and the affirmation of the body do not mean we can focus our lives on sport or other physical pleasures, but they do mean that God created us to move around and enjoy living in these imperfect jars of clay.

One way to think about the importance of our bodies is to consider the concept of play. Most people don't think about "play" at all, since playfulness seems natural and in no need of an explanation. We observe animals being playful. In humans, it seems play is hardwired into us— because it is. On December 26, 2004, a massive earthquake in the Indian Ocean caused a tsunami—a destructive wave of water that unleashed tragic devastation in several countries in the Eastern Hemisphere. Hundreds of thousands of people were killed, and many more people were affected by the loss of their loved ones, homes, and way of life. Many children were left orphaned and traumatized beyond measure. Relief organizations from around the world responded with food, health care, and shelter. But one devoted to children, UNICEF, responded in a unique way. Orphaned children, with looks of shock and fear on their faces, were given "play kits" complete with balls, jump ropes, toys, and games. UNICEF understood what we all know deep inside, that play is powerful and fundamental to human life. Those play kits brought smiles in the midst of disaster, providing diversion in the form of a jump rope.

Playing in the midst of disaster may seem out of place, but that is just the point of play. Play takes us into another world, a world that is imagined and free, a world where everyday stresses and brokenness melt away. Play cannot be coerced. When I was young and my brother and I were causing trouble in the house, we were told to go out and play. We did what we were told and went outside, but we did not immediately begin to play, since to be told to play makes it into something closer to work. Freedom is essential to play.

Play allows us to give meaning to and receive meaning from experiences and circumstances that seem to have little practical relevance. When my children were little, they would spend hours setting up toy houses and acting out the lives of "little people" characters, and I as their dad was corrected if I played in the wrong way. To them, play was serious business. When children play, they are completely sold out to the play world. Time stands still, and the imagined environment is as real as the world around them. Sport has this same play-like quality of make-believe. The world of sport is governed by different rules, and when we enter in, we freely accept the parameters as part of the game.

Play is not only for children; the spirit and action of play are essential for young and old alike. When Jesus told his followers they needed to become like little children, one can surmise that the playfulness of children was part of that message. It is not a stretch to consider our trinitarian God playing as he creates the world, like Aslan singing Narnia into existence in *The Magician's Nephew*. God creates freely and joyfully, as he reminds Job—and us. At creation, "the morning stars sang together and all the angels shouted for joy" (Job 38:7). In creation, "the wings of the ostrich flap joyfully" and "all the wild animals play" (Job 39:13; 40:20). If God creates the world with delight and playfulness, then people made in God's image are also invited to delight and play in it. "All play," wrote philosopher and former Major League Baseball commissioner A. Bartlett Giamatti, "aspires to the condition of paradise."

SUPER SUNDAY

Finally, although a hearty biblical case can be made for work, special care is given in the Bible to the urgency of rest, particularly found in the notion of Sabbath and the feasts and festivals God instituted for the people of Israel. After a pretty productive week, God put a mandatory day of rest on the calendar each week. Its significance was secured in the Ten Commandments, and the New Testament clarified that Sabbath was not for God but for humankind. The Sabbath and other days of rest were implemented for refreshment, freeing us to explore, discover, and take delight in the wonders of God's world. Further, the Sabbath is about relationship. It reminds us of God's covenant to care for us, and in turn, we are reminded to put our full trust in him.

God knew that if left to ourselves, we would become consumed with the unending tasks of life. Sin left a distorting effect on our work, but also on our rest. God is the ultimate provider of both, and problems arise when potentially good things such as play and sport become our god or, more likely, manipulate us to make gods of ourselves.

I often am questioned about the invasion of organized sport into Sunday, since most modern churches declare Sunday as the Sabbath. Superbowl Sunday is fully known by everyone in the United States, and many other professional and amateur sport experiences have what feels like a permanent foothold on Sundays. Sport organizers know that profits grow when more people are off work and can attend and watch events. And because there is no school, youth sports find easy scheduling on Sundays for practices and tournaments. Practically, Sunday is a great day for sports. Yet for people of faith, this leads to two questions. First, is sport itself, whether watching or playing, an activity that echoes a God-intended rhythm of creation and re-creation? Second, is sport's displacement of traditional Sunday observance a sign of misplaced priorities, requiring a call for change?

First, sport is fun and alluring, for players and spectators. Win or lose, participants come back, cementing its allure. We know sport is not perfect delight, perfect freedom, leading to perfect gratitude for our Creator— and sometimes it is far from it. And though the sound of football or golf on TV on a Sunday afternoon puts my wife to sleep, sport does not perfectly meet the definition of godly rest. Yet for most, sport contains moments of delight, portions of joy, occasions for creativity, and opportunity for refreshment. For most, sport participation is voluntary and separate from work, and as such, it can be an enriching diversion in the rhythm of a Christian life, any day of the week.

Yet regarding Sunday observance, Christians are right to revisit and question the place of sport, as the church has done many times in the past. The Christian life is one of both obedience and freedom. And as we reflect on the Sabbath, both Scripture and church tradition present a compelling argument for observing weekly worship with other Christians and setting aside a specific day for rest. But conversely, the Bible also highlights a tendency to find false security in rigid rule following regarding religious practices, such as Sabbath keeping. When speaking of days specifically set aside in the Jewish calendar, the author of Romans says, "One person considers one day more sacred than another; another considers every day alike. Each of them should be fully convinced in their own mind. Whoever regards one day as special does so to the Lord. . . . Whoever abstains does so to the Lord" (14:5–6). This passage points to some flexibility but also steers us toward a discerning process in step with the Holy Spirit.

Today, some Christian schools and colleges choose not to schedule sporting events on Sunday, while others do. Some families choose not to participate in sport on Sundays, while others spend entire summers away from church in favor of travel teams for their children. Leisure expert Paul Heintzman notes that there are both quantitative and qualitative aspects to Sabbath. In short, this means there is both a concrete, measured aspect (quantitative) and a mindful condition of relationship with our God (qualitative). I have found this template to be helpful as I counsel families about sport on Sunday. Often, we need a quantified restriction, discipline, or action to help us truly experience the love of God and overcome the fear of missing out and falling behind. Sometimes decisions to participation in sport on Sunday are made less by joy and more by fear or a desire to prove ourselves. What if I fall behind in my sport? What if I don't practice like everyone else? What if I miss the big game? Conversely, religious rules and practices may lack the assuring aspects of relationship and trust, providing a false sense of security not unlike that of the religious leaders Jesus rebuked so often.

Rigid rules are not likely the best practice, but neither is regular dismissal of communal worship in favor of travel team schedules or professional sport events. It is unlikely there is a simple solution for individuals and communities of faith. Answers and actions are more likely to come from meaningful engagement with Scripture, the Holy Spirit, and fellow Christians. Rest can be inactive, but it can also be avocational, recreational, creative, and expressive. We also know that the changing seasons of life will require continual revisiting of practices and commitments to honoring the Sabbath and living in community with fellow believers. Regardless of large and small choices we make regarding sport and Sunday observance, Christians will not be served by either fear or guilt. Obedience to God will bring a sense of security and freedom, and vice versa, and this will happen in relationship: "Come to me, all you who are weary and burdened, and I will give you rest" (Matthew 11:28).

What about Competition?

4

ANYTHING YOU CAN DO . . .

Sometime around 1950, some surfers in California were bored due to a lack of quality waves, so they put skates on the bottom of a board, and "sidewalk surfing" was born. Throughout the next few decades, the popularity of skateboards exploded. The skateboard culture earned a rough reputation of rebellious kids hanging out and doing drugs, but largely they were just . . . playing. In parking lots and near curbs on street corners, skateboarders would try tricks. As you can imagine, mastering a new trick required equal parts courage and perseverance. When someone could do a trick, others were tempted to follow. "Anything you can do, I can do better." The back-and-forth, lead-and-follow style of skateboard play became a phenomenon. Soon people began to see the potential in harnessing this popularity. The infusion of adult organizers and the possibility of profit led to the development of skateboarding as a sport. Today, organized skateboarding competitions happen all over the world, and skateboarding will be introduced as an Olympic sport for the first time in 2020 in Tokyo.

In Chapter 3, we looked at play and its role in the lives of humans who are made in the image of God. But play and sport, while compatible and often experienced together, are not the same thing. Instead, although sport emerges from our desire to play, sport introduces the desire for excellence, as we saw in Chapter 2, and competition is built into the package. Sport has no corner on competition, of course. Graduates compete for jobs, businesses compete for customers, politicians compete for votes, men and women compete for marriage partners, and churches even compete for congregants. But though similar, the competition of sport is unique.

The skateboarding story illustrates the movement from play to sport. The pleasure of play grows as learned abilities open up new possibilities for action and comparison to others. Some play includes competitive elements, such as the early skaters trying to outdo each other on their boards. But sport and competition are never separated. Sport is competition, so we need to consider carefully how to handle this thing called "competition."

A DODGY RELATIONSHIP

I have a friend from England, and we both fancy the game of golf. Whenever we get together, we play, once even in a snowstorm when the ground was so hard we literally needed to use a hammer to get the tee in the turf. Nick and I are brothers in Christ; we would both say that our Christian faith is central to our lives. Yet during our matches, we would both confess that what we enjoy most is not God's creation or our brotherhood—but whooping each other. We play for this mysterious thing called "bragging rights." After the round, we brag about not only who is a better golfer but also who is a better athlete, from a better country, and so on. Scripture says, "May I never boast except in the cross of our Lord Jesus Christ" (Galatians 6:14). Apparently, that verse left out golf. Sport and Christian faith have a relationship, as they say in England, that is "quite dodgy."

The elephant in the room of sport is competition. The competition of sport makes us, as Christians, uneasy, and it should. On its face, nothing about competition seems, well, Christian! If you do something better than I do and earn victory, you are selfish and potentially harmful to me. My pride is wounded, my self-esteem suffers in comparison, and I may even be humiliated. What is worse, you seem to be happy about it. You may not actually enjoy my pain, but you sure are celebrating it. Put this way, competition seems morally indefensible and spiritually inconsistent with the path of following Christ.

Competition starts with comparison, a practice that does not have a good track record in Scripture. Cain compared his offering with Abel's. When Cain recognized that God favored Abel, Cain killed Abel because of it. Jacob compared his inheritance to Esau's, prompting him to steal it. Comparison opens the door for envy to take up residence in our hearts. Rachel envied Leah's ability to have children, Joseph was envied by his brothers, Saul envied David for his popularity, and David envied Uriah for his wife. The Pharisees tolerated Jesus when he was a small player, but as his ministry and crowds grew, the Pharisees envied him, and the competition was on. Beyond envy, competition seems to be fertile soil for several of the deadly sins, including lust, greed, vanity, anger, and pride. C. S. Lewis called pride "competitive by its very nature." He continued, "Pride gets no pleasure of having something, only out of having more of it than the next man. The pleasure of being above the rest." Doesn't that sound like sport?

It is no surprise that competition in sport mirrors this list of vices, sometimes on a grand scale. For instance, the entire country of Russia was banned by the International Olympic Committee (IOC) from competing in the 2018 Winter Olympic Games in South Korea. The ban was for systematic, state-backed doping among the country's athletes. Ironically, the IOC and other large sport organizations such as FIFA, which manages soccer worldwide, are trying to rehabilitate their images after major corruption scandals. High-profile university sport programs in the USA have recently been caught with tawdry recruiting violations and cover-ups, and stories of teams and individuals who cheat to win seem to come out every day.

IN IT TO WIN IT

In response to these misgivings about competition, some in the Christian community have tailored a response to the "win at all costs" mentality attributed to sport, a response that is ultimately misleading. It is simply this: winning doesn't matter. Here is the argument. Whether I win or lose, I get joy from the experience, the drama and flow of the moment, the satisfaction of getting better, and the accompanying moral and spiritual development. In sport, participation is the prize, and in the end, everybody wins. Since I don't care about the outcome, there is no guilt in winning and no agony in losing. We all finish in the same place, with the same outcomes. The prize is irrelevant.

At first glance, this argument seems compelling. This solves the problem, allowing Christians to participate in sport without the messy problem of self-interest. Except, no matter what we can get our brains to think and our mouths to say, deep down we know better. If we have played a sport, then we know that playing hard, or even playing to the best of our abilities, is a weak substitute for actually winning. Of course, we lose and lose often. Every sport season ends with one winner and a host of losers. But the fact remains that from the beginning, everyone sets out to win.

My oldest daughter is a reader; she consumes fiction. Sometime in her early teens, I happened across her when she got to a certain point in the novel she was reading. She was sobbing uncontrollably. As a caring father full of appropriate empathy, I reminded my teenage daughter that "it's only a book." She was obviously not comforted by my words and was also offended. This book, this make-believe world, mattered deeply to her. The made-up characters were important to her life, and by this time in the book, she was invested in the story. Books move her, change her, delight her, but only because she is willing to give her full self to the story.

In a similar way, if we don't engage, invest, or risk, or if we are unwilling to bear the pain, sport has no chance to move us in any satisfying way. As a sport competitor, I want to bear the jarring, difficult, and sometimes utterly painful feeling of losing to my friend on the golf course on a given day precisely because I want to preserve the possible triumphant, explosive, and sweet jubilation of victory the next time we play. When my son is moping about a loss in sport, I am trained to say, "Get over it. It's only a game." He may need to get over it, and it is a game, but it is not insignificant, because he risked enough to care about the outcome.

For sport, according to sport philosopher Scott Kretchmar, "At the end of the day, possessions matter." We want the trophy, the Green Jacket, the Claret Jug, the Stanley Cup, or the gold medal (even if mine was worth only three dollars). The process of sport matters, but we must acknowledge that the goal of the process is to win. Sport is not sport if it frames winning as simply one among many equal outcomes. We have been taught to say the right things in victory and defeat—"I'm just happy to be here, happy to have the chance"—and in sportsmanlike manner to hide the joy of victory and mute the regret of loss. Sportsmanlike words have merit, but they also have a tinge of inauthenticity, one that the Christian community needs to confront to make sense of sport. As Christians, we can pretend that winning doesn't matter to us, but I don't think the secular world will believe us. Regardless of how many teams or individuals are competing, there is only one prize, and everyone knows it. And in the world of sport, it is valuable. If we don't care who wins, we have violated a central aspect of sport. Sport doesn't work if we don't care.

In his influential book *The Joy of Sports*, Catholic philosopher Michael Novak wrote, "If I had to give one single reason for my love of sports it would be this: I love the test of the human spirit." Novak's "spirit" here refers to the human desire to struggle against the odds, to persevere, with seemingly little hope for success. Without the competitive desire to win, this admirable quality Novak loves so much would be lost. The drama of sport is not only that we don't know the outcome but also that the competitive zeal of a person or, better yet, a team bonding together might just affect the final outcome. Sport provides this opportunity to excel, to push forward in the storm and test ourselves to the edge of our creative capacity.

The desire to win in sport is built into all human beings, even those some might not expect. Eunice Kennedy Shriver recognized this. Troubled by general mistreatment and shunning of people with intellectual disabilities, she started a day camp in 1962 that met in her own backyard. Though not known at the time, Shriver was fueled by the love of her older sister Rosemary, who had an intellectual disability and whose condition was hidden from public view, a common practice at the time. This angered Shriver, and she turned that emotion into a call to action. For many participants, the day camp was the first chance they had to be outside or to play in any public sort of way. Shriver soon discovered that adding sport enhanced the experience for her guests. That camp led to the first Special Olympics Games in 1968, an event that has blossomed to include 5.7 million athletes in 172 countries each year.

But Shriver's vision was not rooted in sentimental sympathy. In a situation in which one might expect a focus on participation, not everyone got a medal. Shriver wanted to provide an authentic competitive experience for the athletes; she wanted them to feel what it was like to strive and win. Of course, all athletes are encouraged and valued, but the joy of winning and the pain of losing are not hidden from Special Olympic athletes. Shriver saw sport competition as humanizing. Special Olympic athletes are expected to train and compete, because that is what sport requires. It was no accident that Shriver chose as a motto a phrase rooted in gladiatorial contests. It unapologetically summarizes the simple attraction of sport: "Let me win, but, if I cannot win, let me be brave in the attempt."

FOUL PLAY

It is a surprise to no one that Christian discipleship does not seem to be a natural by-product of sport competition. Because of the all-consuming fervor inherent with striving for the same goal as someone else, our emotions can get the best of us. The distance between an enriching passion and a destructive obsession is short. Instead of highlighting the best features of humanity, at times sport can seem to draw out the worst. Competition should come with a warning label.

Unfortunately, there is really no shallow end for competition, no training wheels that we can put on until we are ready for the real thing, so we often get it wrong. Though everyone can engage in competition at a moment's notice, our perspectives on it change as we grow and gain experience though trial, error, and reflection. But because we get hurt, get cut, get bored, or become disillusioned, few of us get to a place in sport where we really understand and experience what sport competition is, where it comes from, and what it gives.

Sport competition needs to be learned. There are similarities to other types of competition, but sport competition is different from competing for a job. For most of us, sport competition is almost consequence free. Winning and advancing matter a great deal, but they also don't. Life goes on. The uniqueness of sport is that we can care so much when it matters so little. This is easy to say and hard to do.

Tempering competitive passions requires a healthy detachment, a Christlike perspective, and a lot of practice. Spiritual detachment is not talked about much as a Christian virtue. Detachment may mean withdrawal, but it can also refer to an active engagement in this world with the inner peace that comes from knowing that God is in control. God wants us to be free and to live lives of abundance, seeking him first. In regard to sport, this requires a commitment to mine the motivations of our hearts, rooting out envy and pride and maybe even exposing our desire to cut corners. "The heart is deceitful above all things," wrote the prophet Jeremiah (17:9), reminding us that in sport our hearts have a tendency to dupe us into wrong feelings and actions, especially when much is on the line.

We may have an abstract desire to love God above all, but in truth, we fail over and over. Only God can equip us to love and live according to his purpose, and he tells us to ask him for help. "If any of you lacks wisdom, you should ask God, who gives generously to all without finding fault, and it will be given to you" (James 1:5). God wants to help us with all things, including things that seem as trivial as sport. We can enjoy sport, but as author Gary Thomas puts it, "Ironically, spiritual detachment is the only way to enjoy the physical world, which God made for our pleasure." The only way to truly enjoy sport competition is to let it go, recognizing that we do not own, deserve, or control it. We receive sport in gratitude to our Creator. In sport, we engage our full selves in competition, playing hard to win, but without a Christlike detachment from the results of sport, our appetites will always be unsatisfied.

YOU WIN SOME, YOU LOSE SOME

Sport is held together by shared parameters between opponents. Regardless of the effort and talent a person or a team brings to a contest, chances are the other person or team is bringing the same thing. This is central to sport—teams or individuals comparing performances on a given day or in a season of life. When sport works well, opponents lift one another to higher heights, and each competitor has a responsibility in the process. Of course, some seem to win more than others, but in time, every competitor or team will have their ups and downs. Winning is a primary goal of competition, and Christians need not apologize for it nor pretend winning does not matter. But because there can be only one winner, success defined only by winning is inevitably a losing game.

Sport is often called "zero sum" because there is a clear winner and loser, but that is only partially true. Because sport exists in a make-believe world, the consequences of loss are considered part of the bargain, but so is the chance to play again. Losers do not remain losers forever, nor do winners. They begin again—the next game, the next season, the next year. If we do competition well, recognizing its distinct contribution and limitations, we will more likely see sport competition for what it is, approaching the moment with utmost seriousness yet, in the total story of human life, making less of it, not more.

Competition is a two-sided coin. In both winning and losing, the experience of sport provides opportunities for us to follow our desire to play in a particular way. C. S. Lewis's characters were drawn into Narnia by their own human curiosity; then they threw themselves entirely into the adventure. The adventure included pain and confusion but also the joy of meeting challenges with fresh competence and the satisfaction of doing so alongside others who shared the same passion. Sport is less than we think—it is a form of playacting—but it is also more. The brand of play found in sport is mesmerizing. In moments, it inspires us toward deep gratitude for how we were created. We can imagine the same zeal in God as he thrust the earth into space—not just a boring, functional earth but one of wonder, complexity, and endless capacity for growth. God created us to solve the difficult puzzles, to not settle at good enough, and with the fiery energy needed to live wholeheartedly in this world, because, ultimately, the victory is already his.

Yet even with all its potential delight, I am often asked if every child should play organized sport. My answer is no. Every child should play in some way, since play is part of our nature, but not every child loves organized sport or the type of competition that sport includes, and that is okay. For those who love organized sport, however, it is the opportunity for disciplined, communal, excellent, grueling, exhilarating, intense, dramatic, nail-biting, disheartening, and touching delight.

The documentary *9 Innings from Ground Zero* recounts the well-known tragedy of 9-11, when four airplanes were hijacked by terrorists. Two planes crashed into the Twin Towers of the World Trade Center in New York City, causing both gigantic buildings to collapse on themselves, killing and injuring thousands and shocking the city and the world. In the aftermath, security concerns were high everywhere but especially where large numbers of people gathered, such as Major League Baseball stadiums. Eventually, teams began to play again. By October, the New York Yankees had made it to the World Series, and the entire city was caught up in the excitement. People in the film described how pouring energy into the team with their fellow New Yorkers seemed to have a curative and cathartic effect. Down two games to zero when the series came to New York, the Yankees were able to pull off three dramatic comeback wins in Yankee Stadium. To a mourning city, the team seemed destined to win and to be the soothing balm so desperately needed. But the fairy-tale ending was not to be. The other team, the Arizona Diamondbacks, was still playing to win. Back in Arizona, the Diamondbacks won the final two games of the series quite easily, making them World Series Champions.

The film describes how people turned to faith and family during the tragedy for comfort and answers, but they also turned to baseball for a moment of joy, which they found. They were disappointed the Yankees lost, of course, but were thankful for the momentary diversion and elevated spirit the games provided. They knew baseball was not going to bring back their loved ones or solve the terrorist crisis. They were just looking for a moment of normal human experience in the form of sport.

God's sovereign care extends to all things in creation, including sport. Sport is a contest between people or teams, with both trying their best to win the prize. At its best, sport does carry us away, often in a momentary sense, from the struggles of life, and for that we can be thankful. Sometimes we win, sometimes we lose. And most of the time, we are eager to try again.

Sport Virtues
and Vices

5

TAKE A KNEE

In the United States, it is hard to think of a modern athlete more known for his public Christian faith than football's Tim Tebow. Tebow played college football for the University of Florida, where his team won two national championships, and he was awarded the prestigious Heisman Trophy in 2007. On the field, Tebow regularly pointed skyward after a successful play. His one-knee prayer pose is now known as "Tebowing."

On January 8, 2009, Tebow and his University of Florida team faced Ohio State in the Bowl Championship Series title game to determine the best team in college football. Tebow scrawled John 3:16 in his eye black, a reference to a well-known Bible verse. Statistics show that 90 million people Googled "John 3:16" during the game. But on the same date exactly three years later, something even more astonishing happened. Tebow, then in the NFL with the Denver Broncos, was on the field in what turned out to be the only NFL play-off win of his career. This time another 90 million people Googled "John 3:16," but in addition, Tim Tebow threw for exactly 316 yards, his yards per rush average was 3.16, his average yards per completion was 31.6, the game earned a 31.6 television rating, and the Denver Broncos' time of possession was exactly 31 minutes and 6 seconds.

Cynics, one of whom I have to admit to being in cases like this, easily considered this phenomenon a coincidence. For many, Tebow's outspoken evangelistic style was showy and off-putting. He was criticized for not keeping his prayers private, for proselytizing, and for advancing a single and narrow form of conservative Christianity. Some Christians wondered about the witness of playing a violent game so aggressively with such a fiery zeal for winning while seemingly ignoring the evils of the sport culture. They criticized Tebow for not using his fame to engage in politics or to draw attention to society's problems. As a result, they were rooting against Tebow's success in football because they didn't resonate with his public faith representation.

Yet to others, Tim Tebow was a perfect example of sport and Christianity in full harmony. On the field, he played with grit, tenacity, and an unshakable positive attitude. He spoke openly about his faith to everyone, including the media, and his play seemed almost "blessed." Off the field, he was generous with his time and resources. He spoke to many Christian groups and supported missionaries, including his parents in the Philippines, where he was born. As a famous young man, he was questioned by the media about his life outside of football, namely dating, and he spoke of his conviction not to have sex prior to marriage. To Tebow's supporters, his success represented Christianity's success—and the John 3:16 phenomenon was an endorsement of Tim Tebow's God, who blessed his willingness to use football and his fame to spread the gospel.

Yet I wonder if each of these polarized responses misses the mark. These perspectives stem from an understanding of sport and Christianity that limits both. Each position limits sport because it participates in the timeshare problem we discussed in Chapter 2. Whether in large venues or on small fields, sport is public, and we want to use that public visibility to promote a particular message. Each position also limits Christianity because, through a gesture in sport, we want to control the way people understand the Christian faith and who God is. We want to identify Christianity in and through sport in terms that make sense to us. Our desire to use sport to promote and control a particular message does not honor the integrity of sport or the integrity of our faith.

THROW IN THE TOWEL

An evangelism effort like Tim Tebow's eye black is just one among a number of possibilities that have been offered as a means of making sport more productive and palatable for Christians. Others take a devotional approach to sport, bookending games and practices with team prayer, Bible study, and service projects, often in full display. Still others prefer that Christians apply the rules of sport more strictly than prescribed, calling fouls on themselves or notifying an official when they touched the ball last before it went out of bounds. Some focus on team mission trips or half-time talks for spectators, linking personal sport stories with faith testimonials. A growing segment of the church is drawn to bringing sport to populations on the margins and using it to combat social justice concerns such as race and gender inequality, poverty, and abuse of power. Perhaps most often, Christians are reminded to exercise biblically endorsed traits while playing and watching sports, to practice peace, patience, kindness, and self-control, among other Christian virtues.

We have much to learn from these efforts, since they all spring from a sincere desire to follow Christ in our day-to-day lives, personally and corporately. In Christ, we are new creations; there is evidence to a life of faith. These Christian sport strategies remind us of the primacy of the gospel and our mandate and privilege to make disciples and show God's love to those around us. We are encouraged in Christian practices of prayer and Bible reading, and we are spurred to live lives of holiness.

Yet each of these efforts may be constructing a story that acts as a barrier to an authentic representation of sport and, by extension, the joyous and difficult path of following Jesus Christ. Each of the programmed applications of Christian sport sound to the ear a bit more like work than play—more like busyness than rest. Because of sin, we desire and seek to control sport, sometimes changing it in ways that no longer resemble its true essence. In some ways, when we Christianize sport, we remove the necessity for God. We use him to fuel our competitive advantage, adding a veneer of God's endorsement to a culture less in need of his protection and more in need of his presence.

The experience of sport, as we saw in Chapter 2, is its primary outcome, an experience that God makes possible through the bodies he created and the world in which we live. Sport is a form of playacting. When we give ourselves wholeheartedly to the experience of sport, we are living a little version of ourselves on the stage of sport. So sport does not need to be made artificially "Christian" when played by God's people. We don't need to reduce sport to a set of moral dos and don'ts. We don't need to bookend it with overt Christian practices. When we do these things, when we have our moral and spiritual checklists all figured out, we can easily forget about engaging with God in the process. What we need to do is to play sport the way we live life: depending on our Creator in every moment and in every action.

And that is both liberating and challenging. We are called to be disciples of Jesus Christ in sport as we are in "real" life. That means learning how to love God and neighbor better, how to turn away from thoughts and actions that dishonor God and harm ourselves and others, how both to be wary of our own desires and to delight in the good things that God has made. The good news is that the Christian life isn't difficult . . . it's impossible. We can't "do it right." We can't add up a lot of rules and regulations that will equal "perfect Christian life." Instead, as we walk each day in God's grace, we grow to look more like our Savior. We want it to be said of us, as it was said of the twelve-year-old Jesus, that we are growing "in wisdom and stature, and in favor with God and man" (Luke 2:52).

A GLUTTON AND A DRUNKARD

Sport requires a playful antagonism against one's opponent. For this reason, it is important to remember that what appears self-centered in sport practice and play may not be. Actions taken to win a contest, if within the rules and mores of the game, are a central aspect of the competition. When NBA superstar and self-acknowledged Christian Steph Curry shimmies his shoulders in a celebratory manner after a series of successful three-point shots, he is not only expressing his joy but also sending a message to his competitors. In truth, he wants them to be annoyed, exasperated, and frustrated and to lose competitive confidence—because it will help his team win. Christians are sometimes concerned about such actions in sport. We are somehow okay with a dominant physical performance, but when mental and emotional dominance appears in what we consider to be untoward forms, we are critical, maybe even judgmental—unless of course the player plays for our team. And yet to compete means literally to "strive together." The striving we do in sport is about sport. It frees both sides of a competition to strive toward the goal, the goal to win the contest.

We tend to endorse athletes and coaches who have found a way to be quiet and well mannered inside and outside of sport. But we need to be careful not to categorize this type of demeanor as Christian and the opposite as somehow not. The urgency and the emotion of sport evoke all types of personalities and cultures, and often we cannot sift one from the other. Every athlete and coach is a complex person doing battle in the public sphere and in his or her own heart. For instance, arguably the greatest male tennis player of all time is Roger Federer. Federer is a gentleman's gentleman in a genteel sport. There is even a YouTube video of his sportsmanlike moments when he overrules the umpire making a call in his favor and applauds great plays of his opponents. He is philanthropic with his money, and he supports organizations that help people. But conversely, Federer does not pray before or after tennis matches in any way that others can see, nor does he make gestures that suggest he is honoring God. Federer does not speak about faith on or off the court, and though he doesn't do it much, he will argue with umpires, even cursing on occasion. Federer is considered classy and humble while at the same time remarkably confident and intimidating. He most often says little to his opponents, yet they know he is a master of dominance in his body and mind. He prepares his skills to perform at the most important moments, and his casual, almost dismissive manner provides him with a mental and emotional advantage, one meant to help Federer with the most important task on the secluded island of sport—to defeat his opponent.

In Luke 7, Jesus was described by onlookers as a glutton and a drunkard. It wasn't true, but to outside observers, Jesus was having so much fun that they made inaccurate judgments about his actions and his heart. Can a spectator in the stands spot the Christians on the field? If you didn't know better, a passionate kiss between a man and his wife of twenty years would look no different than one between a man and his secret mistress—even though one celebrates the pleasure of godly romance and the other is an indulgence of a shameful affair. As with sport, from a distance, the kiss looks the same. The difference is most often hidden in the human heart. Roger Federer was born and brought up in the Roman Catholic tradition and still confesses his Christian faith today, but one wouldn't know that without knowing him—or doing a Google search.

The psalmist asks God to search and know his heart. In sport, we are well served to do the same and to listen to what God is telling us. Our desires and affections for sport can open doors for understanding ourselves and God. Living in a deeper relationship with God will provide answers and direction for our biggest questions in sport. Often, a good way to understand something is to explore how it makes you feel. Are my experiences in sport enhancing my relationship with God or tugging me away?

As a coach and an athlete, I have been out of step with God's will for me many times—but I pressed ahead anyway, in my own strength and control. At times, vengefulness, envy, pride, and anger have been the source of my efforts in sport, and I gave into the self-delusion that I was right to take the actions I did. However, I have also had times when my heart was more open and welcoming to the work of the Holy Spirit, and in those moments, my competitive desire to win a contest or pattern my practice toward defeating an opponent did not dissipate. I have won and lost both ways, and I am learning a better way.

God speaks in many ways. The Bible is his Word, and the Holy Spirit can enter in and change us from the inside out. We also live in communities, and fellow believers speak into our lives, giving us counsel when we ask, and sometimes when we don't. In some cases, God speaks directly to us in audible moments. And then there are those apparent coincidences that jolt us from the mundane and provide us with a fresh, if momentary, gratitude toward our Creator.

Once a cynic, I believe Tim Tebow's statistics were no coincidence. What I do not know is how or for what purpose the Holy Spirit made it happen. I suppose an evangelistic purpose or some kind of encouragement to a set of believers is possible, but I am not sure. I am okay with the mystery, but I would like to think that maybe God was playing with us, perhaps even teasing our sensibilities a bit. Maybe he was reminding us that it is okay to take sport seriously but, regarding ourselves, we should lighten up.

A Place
for Sport

6

YOU ARE WHAT YOU LOVE

American author Nathanial Hawthorne wrote a short story entitled "The Great Stone Face." It takes place in a rural valley located in an unnamed town with mountains nearby. From the right distance, a rock formation high above looks like a human face. Because of this unusual feature, a prophetic legend becomes the signature of the town. One day, it is said, a person born within sight of the formation will grow to resemble the great stone face. He will possess great knowledge and wisdom and will be of the most noble character. A young boy in the village named Ernest becomes intrigued with this legend. From the moment he is told the story, Ernest begins gazing at the rock formation every day, studying its features. Ernest longs to meet the person who will resemble the great stone face, and he longs for the prophecy to be fulfilled in his lifetime.

By and by, a merchant from the town who had moved away and made his fortune returns. Given his fame and riches, the townspeople think he surely will be the fulfillment of the prophesy. Ernest too, is eager to see him, so he joins all the townspeople as they gather to welcome their new hero. When they see the merchant in all his grandeur, the people are convinced, but Ernest is not. The merchant's face bears no resemblance to the goodness and wisdom of the great stone face, nor does he turn out to be particularly noble. As time passes, the people understand what Ernest knew from the start, that this man is not the one.

Ernest is disappointed, but he keeps to his tasks, and he keeps studying the rock face. As he grows into adulthood, he becomes a farmer and later a lay pastor. Everyone in the town knows and respects him. But the same pattern with the merchant repeats itself. The next man to appear who might fulfill the legend is a military hero, followed by a superb orator, who is followed by a poet. But each time a man is examined, for one reason or another, he is not the fulfillment of the prophesy. Ernest, however, remains in the town, a respected and beloved person. Every day he keeps gazing at the stone face, and he can almost hear it speaking to him. But as Ernest becomes an old man, he slowly and sadly comes to the realization that the prophesy is not going to be fulfilled in his lifetime.

Over time, Ernest becomes the town expert on the stone face legend. On the occasion of his last sermon, the congregation asks Ernest to deliver his sacred remarks from a site at the base of the notch where the worshipers can see the Great Stone Face high above. As Ernest addresses the crowd, they stare up the stone face, then back at Ernest. Hawthorne describes the climactic scene: "The face of Ernest assumed a grandeur of expression, so imbued with benevolence, that the people threw their arms aloft and shouted, 'Behold! Behold! Ernest is himself the likeness of the Great Stone Face!'" The prophecy was fulfilled. Ernest had fixed his eyes on the image in the rock, and he had become what he loved best.

OUR TRUE IDENTITY

Sport is powerful but many times not in the way we suspect. It can become a powerful love that shapes us into its own image. The Old and New Testament depiction of idols as stone or metal statues does not resonate today because Christians cannot imagine carving an image and bowing down to it. But sport itself has the possibility of being a modern-day idol. Pastor and author Tim Keller defines an idol as "anything more fundamental than God to your happiness, meaning in life, or identity." An idol is a good thing that turns into an ultimate thing—and we are warned that even good things such as family or service to the church can become idols. Like many other human endeavors, sport for children and adults has a way of being all-consuming. Entire families can become intoxicated by sport success or opportunity afforded through sport. When decisions regarding sport compromise deeply held values or require lengthy rationalizations, these are warning signs that sport has moved from appropriate affection to idol.

It is true that the sport culture is loaded with important, authentic, and inspiring stories. At times, sport has the power to uplift or create a new identity. It can be the confidence builder for the disheartened teenage girl who suddenly finds a home on the basketball court. For the fatherless young boy who can run down a fly ball or steal a base to help his team win, sport can provide an alternative community where he does not feel abandoned or rejected. I even know an elderly man who traveled the United States with friends competing in a softball league for old men. He and his family were pleased that he ultimately took his final breath playing the game he loved. But sport can also deform us, when it becomes what we love more than anything or anyone else.

Questioning the depth of our hearts is not easy. As an adopted child of God, I both proclaim and confess to loving sport. As a player, coach, administrator, parent, and spectator, I know that there are times when I relocate sport in my heart from a good thing to an ultimate thing. In those moments, I confess, ask God and others for help, and take steps to change. Like Ernest, I begin to look like that which I love. If I love sport best, my very identity will depend on sport. If I love Christ best, my very identity will depend on him. No one finishes last in a race and is immediately comforted by the knowledge that our identity is in Christ—but it remains true. As we ponder sport and Jesus Christ, we would benefit from turning the mirror on ourselves to see whom we are resembling, and doing so with humble hearts.

EXPLORE YOUR STORY

Now a pastor in Alberta, Canada, Gavin Peacock was first an English professional footballer (soccer player) and later a media analyst. Gavin became a Christian at age eighteen. During most of his professional sport career, his Christian faith was known by his teammates and the wider community. In response to the question about how difficult it was to be both a Christian and a star athlete, he responded, "It's difficult being a Christian in any walk of life."

There is no question that Christians are being watched by the world, no matter what we pursue. But it is also true that sport is visible, and how Christians act in sport is a public testimony for good or ill. Baylor, Penn State, and Michigan State Universities in the United States have been part of very large and public sex abuse scandals involving their athletic programs. In all three cases, the offenses were clearly wrong, but the power of sport won out again. Fearful of public exposure and harm to their athletic programs, the schools failed to shine a light in the darkness—until it was too late. Two public universities, one Christian university, and the results were largely the same. Although the whole world is broken due to the fall into sin—including individuals and systems in sport—Christians are called to repent of their failures, make restitution, and seek to live a more godly life. Christians in sport, as well as in every other area of life, should not look exactly the same as the world.

The early church was wary of sport, and we should be too. Right and wrong are easy to see in sport but often only in retrospect. Perhaps as Christians, we could benefit by thinking less about right and wrong after sport and more about wisdom and folly within sport. A primary point in this book is that the large and small questions involving sport in our lives as Christians require the same kind of careful reflection as other decisions. The answers should flow from our faithful and unending interactions with God and fellow believers. We cannot lay down a simple set of rules to follow to make sport more "Christian." Instead, we need constantly to be examining our loves, our choices, and our time commitments in the light of our desire to grow as Christ's disciples and to look more like him.

One way to begin this examination is to review our own stories past and present with the goal of gaining a better understanding of sport, including why and how it has a place in the life of Christians. To get things started, below is a personal example that includes moments of both folly and wisdom.

THE 24-HOUR RULE

My son was recently participating in a high school sport, and he was not getting a fair opportunity (to my biased eyes). The coach-athlete-parent triad is perhaps one of the most complex in sport. Coaches are not always fair and accurate. Players are not always honest with themselves or others. Parents are sometimes not capable of seeing the big picture or accurately understanding sport decisions. For this reason, coaches often implement what they call a 24-hour rule. If a player or a parent is concerned or upset about something, he or she must allow a day for emotions to settle before addressing it.

In general, I choose not to intervene with my children's coaches, but in this case, I was ready. I started by becoming very angry, filling in motives for the coach that were likely not accurate. I wrote an aggressive letter, detailing all my grievances and indicating how he should change as a coach. I never intended to send it—or maybe I did. Fortunately, due to good counsel from fellow believers, I did not send the letter. Instead, I spoke with my son about the situation, and we prayed for guidance. This was a terrific opportunity for both of us to grow in our understanding of the situation and to remind each other of the proper place of sport. Ultimately, my son decided to talk to the coach himself, and he did so in a way that was not defensive or accusatory. He also did so in private so as not to put the coach in a compromising situation. My son grew in this short exchange, and I think his coach did too. The coach listened and acknowledged some error and lack of communication in the way he was coaching. The two have a better relationship now.

The 24-hour rule is a useful one, whether or not you are a Christian. But I would add this amendment to it. Christians should pray and seek the Holy Spirit's counsel during any discernment time. Sometimes submitting sport concerns to prayer doesn't even occur to us. We rationalize that God has better things to do or that God doesn't care about trivial things such as sport. Yet Scripture clearly says we are not to be anxious *about anything*. Whatever makes us anxious, including sport, can be submitted to God, and the Holy Spirit promises to show up.

It is tempting to finish this story by saying that my son had a great sport experience going forward and that his discussion with his coach cleared up all the problems. But if you love sport and have been around it for a while, you know that things do not often work that way. My son may never get the opportunity he desires in this sport, but the competitive nature of sport makes that true for just about everybody at one time or another. He addressed the situation with humility and strength and in submission to God's will in his life. That is a pretty good ending for now.

CRUNCH TIME

When God made the world, it was good, but in a way, it was unfinished. He made humans to create and fill the world, and beyond work, he intentionally left space for play. One offshoot of play is sport, with its built-in competition, allegiance, and serious striving. Like symphonic music or craft beer, sport is a slice of human existence made from the good stuff God left here.

Sport is a part of ordinary life that does not seem so ordinary. The experience draws us in and brings us back, day after day, season after season. We love to play—and yes, to win, or at least to invest enough of ourselves to have a chance. God's world includes the myth-like space where sport resides, where we celebrate our humanness, our desire to be excellent, and our need to belong. Sport at its best points us toward a future of play and delight. And God is there with us, in every leap, backflip, tackle, spike, and slap shot.

Sport can train us, educate us, change us, for better or for worse, but that is really not the point. First and foremost, sport is part of a truly abundant life for those who love to play. The meaning of sport is not primarily in its use but in its practice. Sport is something we do, something we experience. Yes, sport can be harnessed, often times for good things such as evangelism or personal development, but as with many other human endeavors, the effects beyond what the experience yields are conditional. The point is that because of how we are made, doing sport is an experience like no other. For Christians, resting in God's delight in sport means acknowledging that we are honoring the game, authentically competing, and getting a taste of the freedom that comes for those in Jesus Christ.

God is in control of the world he made, and he sustains it. He calls us to him, and when we respond with our trust, God promises to enter in through his Holy Spirit, equipping us to grow toward him and to participate in his redemption plan, which, for some of us, may include sport.

To be salt and light in sport means we confess our own sin when we fail but also the self-righteousness that can come when we do something well.

When we hear the phrase "the thrill of victory," most who are old enough will finish it with the famous ABC sports motto "and the agony of defeat." This simple phrase sums up the attraction of sport. The experience that is sport brings us to the edge, to that hair-thin, crunch-time moment that will turn our hearts toward momentary thrill or despair. Both emotions are part of human flourishing in and through sport, and for both, we are grateful.

Notes

Series Editor's Foreword

7 **Midway along the journey of our life:** The opening verse of Dante Alighieri, *The Inferno*, trans. Mark Musa (Bloomington: Indiana University Press, 1995), 19.

8 **"We are always on the road":** From Calvin's thirty-fourth sermon on Deuteronomy (5:12–14), preached on June 20, 1555 (*Ioannis Calvini Opera quae supersunt Omnia*, ed. Johann-Wilhelm Baum et al. [Brunsvigae: C. A. Schwetschke et Filium, 1883], 26.291), as quoted in Herman Selderhuis, *John Calvin: A Pilgrim's Life* (Downers Grove, IL: InterVarsity, 2009), 34.

8 **"a gift of divine kindness":** From the last chapter of John Calvin, *Institutes of the Christian Religion, 1541 French Edition*, trans. Elsie Anne McKee (Grand Rapids, MI: Eerdmans, 2009), 704. Titled "Of the Christian Life," the entire chapter is a guide to wise and faithful living in this world.

Chapter 1

16 **a contest or set of contests between teams or individuals:** For a more comprehensive definition of sport, see Allen Guttmann, *From Ritual to Record: The Nature of Modern Sports* (New York: Columbia University Press, 1978).

Chapter 2

23 A story is told: Maeve Louise Heaney, *Music as Theology: What Music says about the Word* (Eugene, OR: Pickwick Publications, 2012), 118.

23 And the experience is why people play sports: A whimsical and delightful explanation of the centrality of games is found in Bernard Suits, *The Grasshopper: Games, Life and Utopia*, reissued ed. (Peterborough, ON: Broadview Press, 2005).

24 For a long time, scholars did not bother to explore or study sport at all: Nick J. Watson, "New Directions in Theology, Church and Sports: A Brief Overview and Position Statement," *Theology* 121, no. 4 (2018): 243-51. For a more comprehensive survey of the literature, see Nick J. Watson and Andrew Parker, *Christianity and Sport: Historical and Contemporary Perspectives*, Routledge Research in Sport, Culture and Society (Abingdon, UK: Routledge, 2012).

24 the importance of sport is really its unimportance: Randolph Feezell, *Sport, Play, and Ethical Reflection* (Urbana: University of Illinois Press, 2004).

25 Sport, for instance, allows us to enter a mythical world: An explanation of the mythical qualities of sport is found in Andrew Cooper, *Playing in the Zone: Exploring the Spiritual Dimensions of Sports* (Boston: Shambhala Publications, 1998).

26 is like walking through the wardrobe with Peter, Susan, Edmund, and Lucy: C. S. Lewis, *The Lion, the Witch, and the Wardrobe* (New York: HarperCollins, 1950).

29 In the movie *Jerry Maguire*: *Jerry Maguire*, directed by Cameron Crowe (Culver City, CA: Sony Pictures Home Entertainment, 1996), film.

30 most people know that winning athletes in ancient Greece: A foundational text on the games of ancient Greece is

Stephen G. Miller, *Ancient Greek Athletics* (New Haven, CT: Yale University Press, 2004).

35 At the highest levels, temptation for cutting corners: For an excellent description of the effects of sin in sport at a personal and systemic level, see Shirl James Hoffman, *Good Game: Christianity and the Culture of Sports* (Waco, TX: Baylor University Press, 2010).

Chapter 3

41 Sport has a universal appeal, and it always has: For a more thorough analysis of sport in the history of the church, see Robert Ellis, *The Games People Play: Theology, Religion, and Sport* (Cambridge, UK: Lutterworth Press, 2014); Lincoln Harvey, *A Brief Theology of Sport* (Eugene, OR: Cascade Books, 2014); and Patrick M. Kelly, *Catholic Perspectives on Sports: From Medieval to Modern Times* (New York: Paulist Press, 2012).

44 They held the Bible in high regard: Leland Ryken, *Worldly Saints: The Puritans as They Really Were* (Grand Rapids, MI: Zondervan, 1986).

45 opening the door for a movement called "Muscular Christianity": For a foundational text on Muscular Christianity, see Tony Ladd and James A. Mathisen, *Muscular Christianity: Evangelical Protestants and the Development of American Sport* (Grand Rapids, MI: Baker Books, 1999).

46 "a human activity of great value, able to enrich people's lives": Pope Francis said these words to participants in the Sport and Faith International Conference, The Vatican, October 5–7, 2016.

48 One way to think about the importance of our bodies is to consider the concept of play: Several scholars have explored play in human life, many from a theological perspective. Here is a partial list: Diane Ackerman, *Deep Play* (New York: Random House, 1999); Johan Huizinga, *Homo Ludens: A Study of the Play-Element in Culture* (1938; reprinted, Kettering, OH: Angelico Press, 2016); Robert K. Johnston, *The Christian at Play* (Eugene, OR: Wipf & Stock, 1997); and Jürgen Moltmann, *Theology of Play* (New York: Harper & Row, 1972).

50 **like Aslan singing Narnia into existence:** C. S. Lewis, *The Magician's Nephew* (New York: HarperCollins, 1955).

50 **"All play . . . aspires to the condition of paradise":** A. Bartlett Giamatti, *Take Time for Paradise: Americans and Their Games* (New York: Bloomsbury USA, 2011), 42.

53 **Paul Heintzman notes that there are both quantitative and qualitative aspects:** Paul Heintzman, William Dyrness, and Robert Johnston, *Leisure and Spirituality: Biblical, Historical, and Contemporary Perspectives* (Grand Rapids, MI: Baker Academic, 2015), 83-106.

Chapter 4

59 **The competition of sport makes us, as Christians, uneasy:** Gary Warner, *Competition* (Elgin, IL: Chariot Family Publishing, 1975).

60 **C. S. Lewis called pride "competitive by its very nature":** C. S. Lewis, *Mere Christianity* (New York: HarperCollins, 2015), 121–22.

62 **"At the end of the day, possessions matter":** This section follows the general argument put forth in Scott Kretchmar, "Competition, Redemption, and Hope," *Journal of the Philosophy of Sport* 31, no. 1 (2018): 101–16.

63 **In his influential book:** Michael Novak, *The Joy of Sports: Endzones, Bases, Baskets, Balls, and the Consecration of the American Spirit*, rev. ed. (Lanham, MD: Madison Books, 1993), 158.

66 **We can enjoy sport:** Gary L. Thomas, *Glorious Pursuit: Embracing the Virtues of Christ* (Colorado Springs: NavPress, 1998), 84.

68 **The documentary *9 Innings from Ground Zero*:** *9 Innings from Ground Zero*, directed by Ouisie Shapiro (New York: HBO Sports, 2004), film.

Chapter 5

74 **For many, Tebow's outspoken evangelistic style was showy and off-putting:** For a media member's perspective on how public gestures of Christianity in sport are perceived, see Tom Krattenmacher, *Onward Christian Athletes: Turning Ballparks into Pulpits and Players into Preachers* (Minneapolis, MN: Rowman & Littlefield, 2009).

75 **An evangelism effort like Tim Tebow's eye black:** For a book critiquing the relationship between Christianity and sport, see William J. Baker, *Playing with God: Religion and Modern Sport* (Cambridge, MA: Harvard University Press, 2007).

Chapter 6

85 **American author Nathaniel Hawthorne :** Nathaniel Hawthorne, *The Great Stone Face Short Story* (1850, reprinted, Fairfield, IA: 1st World Library Literary Society, 2004).

87 **Pastor and author Tim Keller defines an idol:** Tim Keller, *Counterfeit Gods: The Empty Promises of Money, Sex, and Power, and the Only Hope that Matters*, repr. ed. (London, UK: Penguin Books, 2011), xix.

89 **"It's difficult being a Christian in any walk of life":** Gavin Peacock, "Soccer Was My God: Achieving the Goals Wasn't All It Was Cracked Up to Be," *Christianity Today* 60, no. 6 (2016): 95.